Sensual Sips

Table of Contents

Introduction: Sensual Sips- A Journey into Mixology

Choosing the Right Glassware for Your Cocktails..1-2

Essential Bar Equipment for Crafting Perfect Cocktails..3-5

Precision in Mixology: Understanding Cocktail Measurements..................6-8

1. Flirtini: 9
2. Blushing Berry Fizz:... 10
3. Cupid's Cosmo: 11
4. French Kiss:... 12
5. Rosemary Romance:... 13
6. Golden Showers: 14
7. Melted Mingle:... 15
8. Toasted Temptation: 16
9. Back-Shots:...17
10. Skin 2 Skin:.. 18
11. Cozy Cuddle:... 19
12. Sneaky Sip Tini:... 20
13. Shoot My Shot:... 21
14. Risk It All:.. 22
15. Love Potion:.. 23
16. Risqué Rim:... 24

17. Hidden Flame: 25
18. Velvet Vixen: 26
19. XOXO: 27
20. Under the Sheets: 28
21. Rated R: 29
22. Please My Peach: 30
23. Wet: 31
24. Butt Naked: 32

Introduction: Sensual Sips - A Journey into Mixology

Welcome to "Sensual Sips: 24 Cocktails to Keep the Spark in Your Life All 2024" — a tantalizing expedition into the world of mixology designed to add a touch of romance, excitement, and pure enjoyment to your every sip. In these pages, you'll discover not just a collection of cocktails but a sensory experience carefully crafted to elevate the moments that matter

Embarking on a Sensuous Journey:

Mixology is more than the art of crafting cocktails; it's a voyage into the realms of taste, aroma, and emotion. "Sensual Sips" invites you to embark on this journey with us, where each concoction is a chapter in the story of your life — a story enriched with flavors, shared moments, and the art of savoring every drop

24 Cocktails, Countless Experiences:

Within these pages, you'll find a curated selection of 24 cocktails, each with its own unique character, inspired by the essence of love, passion, and self-indulgence. From the spirited effervescence of a "Flirtini" to the warming embrace of a "Cozy Cuddle," each recipe is designed to resonate with the many facets of your relationships, whether they be with your significant other, cherished friends, or the person you value most—yourself.

Beyond the Glass:

This book is not just a guide; it's an invitation to infuse your life with the magic of mixology. We'll explore the art of balancing flavors, the beauty of presentation, and the nuances of selecting the right glassware—all with the aim of turning every cocktail into an experience that lingers on your palate and in your memories.

A Year-Long Celebration:

As we step into 2024, let "Sensual Sips" be your companion in creating moments that transcend the ordinary. Whether you're celebrating milestones, enjoying a quiet night in, or toasting to newfound adventures, these cocktails are crafted to keep the spark alive throughout the year.

Personalize, Indulge, and Savor:

Feel free to make these recipes your own—add your personal touch, experiment with flavors, and share the joy of mixology with those who matter most. Each sip is an opportunity to create a memory, and each cocktail is a chapter in the story of your unique and beautiful life.

So, let the journey begin. May "Sensual Sips" be the catalyst for unforgettable moments, a source of inspiration, and a guide on your path to becoming a true mixologist of love, laughter, and exquisite libations. Cheers to the art of sensual sips and the boundless adventures that await within these pages! *Indulge. Explore. Savor*

Choosing the Right Glassware for Your Cocktails

Selecting the appropriate glassware for your cocktails not only enhances the visual appeal but also contributes to the overall drinking experience. The shape and size of the glass can influence the aroma, temperature, and flavor of the cocktail. Here's a guide to help you choose the perfect glass for each cocktail in our Mixology Experience:

1. Martini Glass:

- Ideal for cocktails like the Flirtini and Sneaky Sip Martini, this classic V-shaped glass allows you to savor the aromas while sipping your elegant and sophisticated concoctions.

2. Highball Glass:

- Cocktails such as the Blushing Berry Fizz and Rosemary Romance are best enjoyed in a highball glass. The tall, narrow shape is perfect for beverages served over ice with a splash of soda.

3. Champagne Flute:

- For effervescent delights like the French Kiss, choose a Champagne flute. The elongated design preserves the bubbles and showcases the visual appeal of your sparkling creations.

4. Rocks Glass:

- Whiskey-based cocktails like the Golden Showers and Toasted Temptation find their home in a rocks glass. The short, wide design is perfect for drinks served over ice or stirred with minimal dilution.

5. Heatproof Mug:

- Perfect for warm and indulgent treats like the Melted Mingle, a heatproof mug ensures your hot cocktails stay warm while providing a cozy and comforting feel.

6. Coupe Glass:

- The Love Potion and Velvet Vixen shine in a coupe glass. This shallow, broad-rimmed glass is perfect for cocktails served without ice, allowing the aromas to blossom

7. Collins Glass:

- Ideal for long and refreshing drinks like the Cotton Candy Kiss, the Collins glass is tall and slender, making it suitable for beverages with a higher volume of mixers.

8. Shot Glass:

- For daring concoctions like the Rated R and Hidden Flame, a standard shot glass is the go-to choice. Perfect for small, intense sips

Remember, the right glass not only enhances the visual appeal but also contributes to the overall enjoyment of your crafted cocktails. Consider the characteristics of each glass type and elevate your Mixology Experience to new heights!

Essential Bar Equipment for Crafting Perfect Cocktails

Behind every great cocktail is a well-equipped bar. Having the right tools on hand not only makes the mixing process smoother but also adds a professional touch to your Mixology Experience. Here's a list of essential bar equipment to ensure you're ready to craft the perfect cocktails:

1. Cocktail Shaker:

- An absolute must-have for shaking up cocktails like the Flirtini and Sneaky Sip Martini. Choose a quality shaker with a built-in strainer for seamless pouring.

2. Muddler:

- For drinks like the Blushing Berry Fizz, a muddler is essential for gently crushing fruits, herbs, or spices to release their flavors.

3. Bar Spoon:

- Essential for stirring cocktails like the Golden Showers and Toasted Temptation with precision. A long-handled bar spoon ensures thorough mixing without over-dilution.

4. Jigger:

- Achieve the perfect pour for accurate measurements with a jigger. This is crucial for balancing flavors in cocktails such as the Cupid's Cosmo and Love Potion.

5. Strainer:

- A Hawthorne strainer is indispensable for filtering out ice and other ingredients when pouring cocktails from the shaker to the glass, as needed for drinks like the Rosemary Romance.

6. Citrus Squeezer:

- For cocktails requiring fresh citrus juice, like the French Kiss and Rated R, a sturdy citrus squeezer ensures you extract every drop of flavor

7. Ice Bucket and Tongs:

- Keep your cocktails perfectly chilled by having an ice bucket and tongs on hand. Ideal for drinks served in rocks glasses like the Melted Mingle.

8. Blender:

- Essential for creating smooth and blended cocktails like the Cotton Candy Kiss. Ensure your blender is powerful enough to crush ice for that perfect texture.

9. Bar Knife

- A sharp, quality bar knife is essential for garnishing drinks. Use it for cutting fruit twists, pineapple wedges, or any other garnishes for your cocktails.

10. Fine Mesh Strainer:

- For cocktails that require a silky texture, such as the Hidden Flame, a fine mesh strainer is crucial for removing small particles and ensuring a smooth sip

11. Bar Mat and Towels:

- Keep your workspace clean and organized with a non-slip bar mat. Have plenty of bar towels on hand for quick cleanups between cocktails.

Having these essential tools at your disposal will not only make your Mixology Experience seamless but also elevate the craftsmanship of each cocktail. Equip your bar with precision, and let the mixing magic begin!

Precision in Mixology: Understanding Cocktail Measurements

Creating the perfect cocktail is an art that requires precision and balance. The measurements of each ingredient play a crucial role in achieving the desired flavor profile. Here's a guide to the standard measurements (in ounces) used in our Mixology Experience cocktails:

1. Ounce (oz):

- The basic unit of measurement for liquid ingredients in cocktails. It provides a standard reference point for consistency across recipes

2. Jigger Measurements

- Common jigger measurements include:

- 1 oz / 2 oz: Ideal for accurate measuring, ensuring a balanced mix of ingredients.

- 0.5 oz / 1 oz: Useful for smaller quantities, such as flavor modifiers or liqueurs.

3. Cocktail Shaker Capacity:

- Shakers typically come in two sizes:

- Standard Shaker (16 oz): Suitable for most cocktails, including those with a few ingredients.

- Large Shaker (28 oz): Ideal for cocktails requiring more mixing space or additional ingredients.

4. Muddler Increment:

- When muddling ingredients, use gentle pressure to extract flavors. A quarter to half an ounce (0.25 - 0.5 oz) is often sufficient

5. Dash and Splash:

- Not measured in ounces, but rather a quick pour or a few drops:

- Dash: A small amount, typically equivalent to around 1/8 of an ounce.

- Splash: A quick pour, often used for non-alcoholic mixers.

6. Citrus Squeezing:

- The juice of one medium-sized citrus fruit (lemon, lime, or orange) generally yields about 1 ounce of juice.

7. Layering with Precision:

- When layering ingredients, pour slowly over the back of a spoon to control the flow, creating distinct layers

8. Rim Garnish Touch:

- Ingredients like salt or sugar for rimming glasses are often applied sparingly. Use a saucer or plate to catch excess and prevent over-seasoning.

9. Garnish Portions

- Garnishes are not only for aesthetics but also contribute to aroma and flavor. Use small portions, such as a twist of citrus or a few berries

10. Adjusting to Taste:

- Mixology is an art, and personal preferences vary. Feel free to adjust ingredient quantities based on individual taste preferences.

Understanding these measurements ensures consistency and precision in crafting each cocktail. Embrace the art of mixology by mastering the balance of flavors and creating a memorable experience with every sip.

1. Flirtini

- Ingredients:
    1. 2oz Vodka
    2. 1oz Champagne
    3. 1oz Pineapple Juice
    4. 0.5oz Triple Sec
- Garnish: Pineapple wedge or twist of orange peel
- Directions:
    1. In a shaker with ice, combine vodka, pineapple juice, and triple sec.
    2. Shake well and strain into a chilled martini glass.
    3. Top with champagne.
    4. Garnish with a pineapple wedge or twist of orange peel.

2. Blushing Berry Fizz

- Ingredients:
    1. 2oz Gin
    2. Handful of Mixed Berries
    3. 0.5oz Raspberry Liqueur
    4. 0.75oz Lemon Juice
    5. Club Soda
- Garnish: Fresh berries and a sprig of mint
- Directions:
    1. Muddle mixed berries in the bottom of a shaker.
    2. Add gin, raspberry liqueur, and lemon juice.
    3. Shake well and strain into a highball glass filled with ice.
    4. Top with club soda and garnish with fresh berries and a sprig of mint.

3. Cupid's Cosmo

- Ingredients:
    1. 2oz Vodka
    2. 1oz Cranberry Juice
    3. 0.5oz Triple Sec
    4. 0.75oz Lime Juice
- Garnish: Lime twist or cranberries
- Directions:
    1. In a shaker with ice, combine vodka, cranberry juice, triple sec, and lime juice.
    2. Shake well and strain into a chilled martini glass.
    3. Garnish with a lime twist or cranberries.

4. French Kiss

- Ingredients:
    1. 1.5oz Chambord
    2. 3oz Champagne
    3. 0.5oz Raspberry Puree
- Garnish: Fresh raspberries
- Directions:
    1. Pour Chambord and raspberry puree into a champagne flute.
    2. Top with chilled champagne.
    3. Garnish with fresh raspberries.

5. Rosemary Romance

- Ingredients:
    1. 2oz Gin
    2. 0.5oz Rosemary Syrup
    3. 1oz Grapefruit Juice
    4. Soda Water or Sprite
- Garnish: Rosemary sprig and grapefruit twist
- Directions:
    1. In a shaker with ice, combine gin, rosemary syrup, and grapefruit juice.
    2. Shake well and strain into a highball glass filled with ice.
    3. Top with soda water or sprite and garnish with a rosemary sprig and grapefruit twist.

6. Golden Showers

- Ingredients:
    1. 2oz Gold Tequila
    2. 3oz Pineapple Juice
    3. 0.75oz Lime Juice
    4. 0.5oz Agave Syrup
- Garnish: Pineapple wedge and edible golden glitter
- Directions:
    1. In a shaker with ice, combine gold tequila, pineapple juice, lime juice, and agave syrup.
    2. Shake well and strain into a rocks glass filled with ice.
    3. Garnish with a pineapple wedge or edible gold flakes.

7. Melted Mingle

- Ingredients:
    1. 1oz Spice Rum,
    2. 1oz Caramel
    3. 4oz Hot Apple Cider
- Garnish: Whipped cream and cinnamon sprinkle
- Directions:
    1. In a heatproof mug, combine spice rum, hot apple cider, and caramel.
    2. Stir well and top with whipped cream and cinnamon sprinkles.

8. Toasted Temptation

- Ingredients:
    1. 2oz Fireball Whiskey
    2. 1oz RumChata
    3. 0.5oz Toasted Marshmallow Syrup (optional)
- Garnish: Toasted marshmallow on a skewer
- Directions:
    1. In a shaker with ice, Fireball whiskey, RumChata, and toasted marshmallow syrup (optional).
    2. Shake well and strain into a lowball glass.
    3. Garnish with a toasted marshmallow on a skewer.

For The Rim: Mix cinnamon and brown sugar

9. Back-Shots

- Ingredients:
    1. 1oz Amaretto
    2. 1oz Baileys
- Garnish: Whip cream
- Directions:
    1. Pour amaretto, and baileys into a shot glass
    2. Garnish with whip cream.

10. Skin 2 Skin

- Ingredients:
    1. 1oz Kahlua
    2. 1oz Baileys
    3. Float with Grand Marnier
- Directions:
    1. Pour kahula into a double shot glass.
    2. Gently pour in the baileys over the back of a spoon, allowing it to float at the top of the kahlua.
    3. Gently pour the grand marnier over the back of a spoon.

stir all three ingredients before drinking

11. Cozy Cuddle

- Ingredients:
    1. 2oz Baileys
    2. 1oz Cognac
- Garnish: Grated nutmeg and whip cream (optional)
- Directions:
    1. In a lowball glass, combine Baileys, Cognac, over ice.
    2. Top with grated nutmeg.

12. Sneaky Sip Tini

- Ingredients:

    1. 2oz Kettle One Botanical Grapefruit & Rose Vodka or Grapefruit Vodka
    2. 1.5oz Peach Schnapps
    3. 1oz Pineapple Juice
    4. Splash of simple syrup or grenadine (both are optional)

- Garnish: Grapefruit twist
- Directions:

    1. In a shaker with ice, combine grapefruit vodka, peach schnapps pineapple juice, and a
    2. Splash of simple syrup or grenadine.
    3. Shake well and strain into a chilled martini glass.

13. Shoot My Shot

- Ingredients:
    1. Dusse' or any Cognac
    2. Stella Rosa Black

- Directions:
    1. In a shaker with ice, combine cognac, and stella rosa black.
    2. Shake well and strain into a shot glass.

14. Risk It All

- Ingredients:
    1. 1oz Tequila Reposado
    2. 1oz Cointreau or Triple Sec
    3. ½oz Squeeze Lime Juice
    4. ½oz Simple Syrup
    5. Fill with Stella Rosa Blueberry
- Garnish: Edible flower and Lime Wedge
- Directions:
    1. In a shaker with ice, combine tequila, cointreau or triple sec, lime juice, and simple syrup.
    2. Shake well and strain into a rocks glass filled with ice.
    3. Top with stella rosa.
    4. Garnish with an edible flower and lime wedge.

15. Love Potion:

- Ingredients:
    1. 1.5oz Raspberry Vodka
    2. 1oz Chambord
    3. 0.5oz Lime Juice
    4. Splash of Cranberry Juice
- Garnish: Raspberries
- Directions:
    1. In a shaker with ice, combine raspberry vodka, Chambord, lime juice, and a splash of cranberry juice.
    2. Shake well and strain into a chilled martini glass.
    3. Garnish with raspberries.

16. Risqué Rim

- Ingredients:
    1. 2oz Tequila
    2. 1oz Triple Sec
    3. 0.75oz Lime Juice
    4. Salt for rimming
- Garnish: Lime wheel
- Directions:
    1. Rim a chilled martini glass with salt.
    2. In a shaker with ice, combine tequila, triple sec, and lime juice.
    3. Shake well and strain into the salt-rimmed glass.
    4. Garnish with a lime wheel.

** splash of sweet and sour (optional)**

17. Hidden Flame

- Ingredients:
    1. 1.5oz Mezcal
    2. 0.5oz Aperol
    3. 0.75oz Grapefruit Juice
    4. 0.25oz Agave Syrup
- Garnish: Grapefruit twist
- Directions:
    1. In a shaker with ice, combine mezcal, aperol, grapefruit juice, and agave syrup.
    2. Shake well and strain into a rocks glass filled with ice.
    3. Garnish with a grapefruit twist.

18. Velvet Vixen

- Ingredients:
    1. 1oz Vodka
    2. 1oz Tequila
    3. 1oz Rum
    4. 1oz Gin
    5. ½oz of Triple Sec
    6. Splash of Sweet & Sour
    7. Fill with Lemonade
    8. Top with Raspberry Liquor
- Garnish: Edible violet and lemon
- Directions:
    1. In a shaker with ice, combine vodka, tequila, rum, gin, triple sec, and sweet & sour.
    2. Shake well.
    3. Pour into a Highball glass.
    4. Fill to the top with Lemonade with a float of raspberry liquor.
    5. Garnish with an edible violet and lemon.

19. XOXO

- Ingredients:
    1. 2oz Coconut Rum
    2. 1oz Pineapple Juice
    3. 0.5oz Grenadine
    4. Splash of Orange Juice
- Garnish: Pineapple leaf and a cherry
- Directions:
    1. In a shaker with ice, combine coconut rum, pineapple juice, grenadine, and a splash of orange juice.
    2. Shake well and strain into a chilled martini glass.
    3. Garnish with a maraschino cherry.

20. Under the Sheets

- Ingredients:
    1. 1oz Tequila
    2. 1oz Cognac
    3. 0.5oz Blue Curacao
    4. 1oz Sprite
    5. 1oz Pineapple Juice
- Garnish: Grated white chocolate
- Directions:
    1. Pour into a high ball glass filled with ice, tequila, blue curacao, pineapple juice, and cognac.
    2. Stir well.
    3. Top with sprite.

21. Rated R

- Ingredients:
    1. 1oz Tequila or Vodka
    2. 0.5oz Lavender Syrup
    3. Lime Squeeze
    4. 1.5oz Lemonade
- Garnish: Lemon twist
- Directions:
    1. In a shaker with ice, combine tequila, lime squeeze, and fill with lemonade.
    2. Shake well and strain into a chilled Martini glass.
    3. Gently pour lavender syrup over the back of a spoon, allowing it to float on top.
    4. Garnish with a lemon twist.

22. Please My Peach

- Ingredients:
    1. 2oz Vodka
    2. 1oz Peach Schnapps
    3. 0.5oz Lime Juice
    4. Splash of Prosecco
- Garnish: Peach slice
- Directions:
    1. In a shaker with ice, combine vodka, peach schnapps, and lime juice.
    2. Shake well and strain into a chilled highball glass filled with ice.
    3. Top with a splash of Prosecco.
    4. Garnish with a peach slice.

23. Wet

- Ingredients:
    1. 1.5oz Coconut Rum
    2. 1oz Blue Curaçao
    3. 0.75oz Pineapple Juice
    4. Splash of Coconut Cream
- Garnish: Pineapple leaf
- Directions:
    1. In a shaker with ice, combine coconut rum, blue curaçao, pineapple juice, and a splash of
    2. coconut cream.
    3. Shake well and strain into a chilled highball glass filled with ice.
    4. Garnish with a pineapple leaf.

24. Butt Naked

- Ingredients:
    1. 1.5oz Watermelon Vodka
    2. 0.75oz Lime Juice
    3. 0.5oz Simple Syrup
    4. Splash of Grenadine and Sprite
- Garnish: Watermelon wedge
- Directions:
    1. In a shaker with ice, combine watermelon vodka, lime juice, and simple syrup.
    2. Shake well and strain into a chilled highball glass filled with ice.
    3. Top with a splash of grenadine and sprite.
    4. Garnish with a watermelon wedge.

Subscribe To My YouTube Channel

Made in the USA
Columbia, SC
17 October 2024